Original title:
Home Beneath the Roof

Copyright © 2025 Creative Arts Management OÜ
All rights reserved.

Author: Rosalie Bradford
ISBN HARDBACK: 978-1-80587-183-5
ISBN PAPERBACK: 978-1-80587-653-3

Whispered Connections

In the corner, cats convene,
Plotting ways to steal the scene.
Dog barks loud, but they just yawn,
Planning tricks from dusk 'til dawn.

Socks in drawers weave tales untold,
One red, one blue—how bold!
Lost keys dance in shadows, it's true,
Where could they be? Who even knew?

Stanzas of Togetherness

Pancakes flip and syrup drips,
Waffle battles, no one trips.
Milk mustache on Auntie Jane,
Laughter rings, no room for pain.

The disco ball above the sink,
Washing dishes, we all wink.
Grandpa's tunes just make us sway,
Every Sunday, we'll dance away.

The Ties That Hold

Strings of yarn and puppet shows,
Making pals from just a hose.
Mom yells out to close the door,
But we sneak out, want to explore.

The fridge hums with secrets galore,
Leftovers once loved, now a chore.
But in the chaos, there's a spark,
Together we laugh, until it's dark.

Refuge of Hope

Under the table, we huddle tight,
An adventure's waiting just tonight.
Cheese and crackers, a feast for two,
Imaginary friends, they join the crew.

The clock ticks loud, but who's to care?
Time means nothing when joy is rare.
We build a fort with every chair,
In our cozy world, love fills the air.

Foundations of Trust

We built a love on waffles, so doughy and sweet,
A pancake foundation, where syrup's a treat.
Through spills and splatters, we always survive,
With laughter in corners, our joy's so alive.

The cat runs with vigor, the dog steals a sock,
Together they bicker, a hilarious flock.
In chaos we thrive, our laughter's the plan,
We'll dance in the kitchen, a wobbly band.

Memory-Makers

In the attic, we find our grand treasures ablaze,
A polka-dot shirt from the most awkward phase.
Glitter and glue from a long-ago craft,
Reciting old stories, we can't help but laugh.

The tickle fight moments, the food fight of yore,
A ceiling fan whirring, we giggle and snore.
With each cherished memory, our laughter we stir,
We'd rather tell jokes than talk about the blur.

Cherished Shadows

The shadows have secrets, they dance on the wall,
Proclaiming their mischief, the antics of all.
A cat makes a castle; a dog's on a throne,
In this ticklish realm, they feel perfectly home.

We've made a tradition of socks on the floor,
Where mismatched old pairs are now merely folklore.
With laughter our armor, together we stand,
As shadows and light play in whimsical land.

Cradled by the Elements

The wind whispers softly, a tale made of cheer,
While rain drops in rhythms like laughter we hear.
Sunshine arrives, bringing warmth to our skin,
As leaves toss confetti, let the revelry begin!

In the kitchen, we're mixing the flavors of fun,
With flour on foreheads, we battle and run.
Each moment a bubble, each giggle a gust,
In this symphony of chaos, together we trust.

Where Footsteps Resonate Softly

In the hallway, a squeak persists,
Cats prance, dodging misfit lists.
Mom's lost her glasses in plain sight,
And Dad's fallen asleep in the light.

Fridge whispers secrets, old and bold,
Leftovers do stories, never told.
The dog thinks it's a race to the door,
While laughter echoes, begging for more.

The Glisten of Time Well Spent

On Sunday, pancakes fly with cheer,
Syrup rivers flood without fear.
Squeaky chairs sing the morning tune,
As kids argue who'll eat the last spoon.

Chasing shadows with a playful bat,
Grandma's cat thinks it's a fun chat.
Juggling socks like they're popcorn balls,
The dance of chaos forever calls.

Keeper of Secrets and Smoke

In the kitchen, a pot spills stories,
As Dad tries to share his glories.
Mom's magic herbs make the air sway,
While smoke signals whisk worries away.

Beneath the table, treasures lay,
Forgotten crayons in disarray.
The dog winks with a clandestine grin,
And mischief brews where laughter begins.

A Tapestry of Lives Interlaced

With mismatched chairs and plates in stacks,
We're artists at work, in living tracks.
Frog pajamas clash with mom's style,
Yet hugs and chaos are all worthwhile.

When the door swings wide with a hearty bang,
Neighbors peek in, the laughter clangs.
Impromptu plays and faux magic tricks,
We weave our days like the best of flicks.

Pillows of Serenity

In a heap they lie, so soft and bright,
The cat claims one, oh what a sight!
A fortress built with giggles and purrs,
Who knew they'd serve as battle spurs?

Tossed on the couch, they dance and play,
Holding secrets of the day to day.
With snacks and dreams all tucked inside,
A comfy realm where quirks abide.

Echoes in the Hallway

Echoes bounce like rubber balls,
Chasing feet through cozy halls.
Laughter rings, a cat meows,
While shadows plot with silly vows.

A rogue sock hides by the stair,
Planning heists without a care.
Doorknobs giggle as they swing,
In this space, oddities cling.

The Warmth Within

A kettle hums a merry tune,
While socks plot wars by the light of the moon.
Chairs squeak secrets, tales of flair,
Each creak a giggle, lifting despair.

Bouncing between laughter and sighs,
A cushion whispers cautious lies.
Mismatched mugs join for a toast,
To all the joys we love the most.

Solace in the Structure

Walls wear memories like a coat,
Squirrels outside take turns to gloat.
Inside, the chaos is fully alive,
As plants conspire with dust bunnies to thrive.

Cracks in the ceiling form their own art,
A gallery made of goofy heart.
In every corner of this mad space,
Laughter and love weave a warm embrace.

Loving Arms of Hearth and Heart

In the kitchen, cookies burn,
Cat leaps high, a wild turn.
Mom yells loud, it's chaos fun,
Dad just laughs, 'Another one!'

Grandma's knitting, yarn's a mess,
Dog is tangled, what a stress!
Uncle's jokes make no great sense,
Yet they bring us this immense.

Windows to Remnants of Joy

Through the panes, kids run and play,
Splashing puddles on a gray day.
Socks on feet that don't quite match,
Fancy hats from a yard sale batch.

Laughter echoes, voices blend,
Every corner, stories send.
Jars of jelly line the shelf,
'Who ate the last one?' asks ourselves.

The Untold Stories of Our Land

In the garden, veggies grow,
But look out for the sneaky crow.
He steals carrots, oh, what a sight,
Chasing him is quite a fight!

The shed holds treasures old and weird,
A lawnmower that hasn't steered.
Old bikes rusted, tires flat,
Finders, keepers! How about that?

Canvas of Dreams Beneath Starlit Skies

On the porch, we weave our tales,
The night's a friend, it never fails.
Fireflies flicker, stars align,
A s'more here, a giggle thine.

Crickets chirp a symphony,
Nonsense jests from you to me.
Wrap it all in laughter's plot,
In this space, we've got a lot.

Roots Intertwined with Love

In the garden where laughter grows,
Socks on the line, who knows where it goes?
Granddad's old chair, it squeaks and it sways,
While the cat naps and basks in sunrays.

Branches so tangled, a puzzle of fate,
Mom's secret cookies, served way too late.
Every new giggle unlocks a new tale,
Family and chaos, we blissfully sail.

Hearthstone Memories Unraveled

The fire crackles, mischief ignites,
Dad tells a story that just isn't right.
Marshmallows roast, a gooey delight,
Until cousin Mike starts a playful fight.

Pants and socks flying around in the air,
Dance like a chicken, no one seems to care.
The warmth of our laughter fills every nook,
Time spent together, that's all it took.

Lanterns Lighting the Night

Lanterns flicker as shadows take flight,
Siblings sneak snacks, a mischievous bite.
A ghost in the garden? It's just old Tim,
Tripped on the hose, can't help but just grin.

Stories collide like a playful old rhyme,
Under the glow, we forget about time.
Chasing the moonbeams, the oddest of sights,
We joyfully wander on whimsical nights.

The Warmth Within Unfolded

Winter chill bites, but we're snug like bugs,
Pants on the radiator, oh what a snug!
Mom's soup is a treasure, but don't touch my bread,
Or face a pillow fight, right here on the bed!

An odd little dance while we wait for the stew,
Dad tries to beatbox; it's good, but it's new.
Cozy confusion, all wrapped up in glee,
In this joyful chaos, we just let it be.

Cozy Corners of the Heart

In the nook, the cat naps wide,
While socks and shoes together hide.
Pancakes flipped with a messy cheer,
We giggle, spill syrup, never fear.

The clock ticks loud with its silly chime,
Mom's dance moves—oh, they're so sublime!
There's always a secret stash of treats,
Like finding gold beneath your seats.

Old chairs creak like they're telling tales,
Of silly fights and rhymes that fail.
The fridge hums songs of yesterday's dish,
A family feast we all can't miss.

Laughter echoes, bright and loud,
In our quirky, loving crowd.
Cluttered bliss, our joyful scene,
Where every day feels like a dream.

Nurturing Atmospheres

Plants grow wild, with dreams unfurled,
In our jungle, it's a leafy world.
Spilled milk and laughter fill the air,
A dance party starts without a care.

Mom says 'No' but we say 'Yes!'
To midnight snacks—oh, what a mess!
Blankets become forts in the night,
As we plot new adventures, full of flight.

The dog joins in, he's our true friend,
With wagging tail, he'll defend.
While we concoct our grand escape,
In our fortress, there's no room to gape.

Warmth wraps us like a cozy hug,
In our patchwork world, we snug.
Each corner filled with silly joys,
Creating memories, oh what noise!

The Canvas of Us

With crayons we sketch our day to day,
On walls that laugh, they're never gray.
Our fridge showcases art, a grand show,
With magnets that twirl and sometimes glow.

The kitchen's a canvas, chaos reigns,
Where spaghetti tangles in silly chains.
Dishes become mountains, yet we don't mind,
It's here that joy and love unwind.

Pillow forts rise high with pride,
A world where hopes and dreams collide.
With popcorn kernels as our choice,
We gather 'round, rejoicing in voice.

Our lives painted in bright, bold hues,
Each stroke a giggle, a feeling we choose.
In every mess, there's a masterclass,
As family laughter makes moments last.

Roots in the Walls

In the cracks, a plant pops through,
It waves its leaves for a peek at you.
Dust bunnies play hopscotch on the floor,
While children giggle and beg for more.

Under the stairs, secrets are stored,
A treasure chest where dreams are bored.
Silly songs echo from every room,
As socks disappear, with no hint of gloom.

With every bump and creak at night,
Stories bubble with sheer delight.
The family ghost just wants to play,
With silly tricks that light our way.

We gather close for tales so grand,
Where laughter weaves through every hand.
Our house may wobble, but never falls,
Life thrums within these heart-filled walls.

Lanterns of Laughter

A cat in the sink, what a sight to see,
It stares at the fish, thinks 'You're dinner for me!'
The dog steals my socks, they're now his new toys,
In a world full of chaos, we find silly joys.

The kids on the trampoline leap with pure glee,
They launch to the sky, aiming high like a bee.
The microwave beeps, it's a dance in the night,
We gather and laugh, caught up in delight.

Resilient Roots

The plants in the corner grow sideways with pride,
They twist and they turn, on a wild, silly ride.
We water them daily, they flirt with the dust,
In this jungle of life, we just giggle and trust.

A chair with three legs always wobbles around,
It tips like a dancer, with no solid ground.
Yet we lounge on the couch, with snacks by our side,
Finding joy in the quirks that this place cannot hide.

Windows to the Soul

The neighbor sings loud, in a pitch most bizarre,
We peek through the curtain, laughing from afar.
His dog joins the chorus, a howling delight,
With windows wide open, we embrace the night.

The weather is weird, with rain and with sun,
Umbrellas are flipped; oh, this is such fun!
We dance in the puddles, splash water around,
In this crazy old space, pure joy can be found.

Threads of Belonging

A quilt patched together with love and some stains,
Each scrap tells a story, laughs echo like trains.
Grandma's old sweater, where moths had a feast,
Yet wrapped in its warmth, we find joy increased.

The family dog rolls in mud, what a show,
He leaps with a smile, muddy paws all aglow.
As we wash our hands in a splash of good cheer,
In these threads of our lives, we stitch laughter here.

The Nest We Build

In our cozy nook, we squawk and play,
Making messes in wild disarray.
Plates stacked high, a towering feat,
Who knew cereal could be such a treat?

Pillows become mountains, oh what fun!
We dive right in, and no need to run.
With laughter echoing, we create our tune,
The living room's now our cartoon!

Hearthside Reflection

Socks in the dryer, a fashion trend,
Who knew laundry could be such a blend?
Dust bunnies dance like they own the show,
We cheer them on, with giggles aglow.

Chairs all crooked, the table askew,
We make up stories of the lives they knew.
Conversations flow like the coffee pot's drip,
With crumbs of laughter on each steady sip.

Safe Utopias

In our fortress of snacks, we fortify,
With cookie crumbs strewn, oh my, oh my!
The couch is a ship, we sail with glee,
Navigating the oceans of TV spree.

Remote as our compass, we venture so bold,
Charting the realms of sitcoms untold.
Pirates of pizza, a treasure so near,
In this quirky kingdom, we have no fear!

Gables of Compassion

Under the eaves, where the shadows play,
We tell our tales, brightening the day.
A cat on the windowsill, life of the house,
Turns all our whispers into a rouse.

In the garden of giggles, we plant our dreams,
Wobbling like toddlers, or so it seems.
Friendship's a blanket, stitched with delight,
We cuddle up close, 'til the morning light.

Where the Heart Finds Rest

In the corner lies my cat,
Who thinks she's more than just a brat.
She rules the couch with lazy grace,
And claims each cushion as her place.

The fridge hums a cheerful tune,
Where leftovers dance like a cartoon.
A sock collection greets my feet,
A mystery of crumbs and meat.

The door creaks like an old ballet,
Where strangers might just roll away.
The tiny plants are plotting schemes,
To steal the light and chase their dreams.

With laughter echoing through the halls,
This rabbit warren never stalls.
In every crevice, stories weave,
Just watch the chaos and believe.

Under the Canopy of Dreams

The ceiling's paint is peeling bright,
Oh, what a curious sight!
The light bulb flickers like a star,
While socks escape from near and far.

Cushions stacked like little towers,
Fortresses built to test their powers.
Pillow fights erupt at eight,
A sound that rivals any plate.

The plants are snickering in their pots,
While I ignore the little spots.
With every laugh and spilled surprise,
The dust bunnies hold their alibis.

In chaos' arms, we find our way,
Where silliness keeps gloom at bay.
This wacky realm, so full of fun,
Is where our hearts shall always run.

Sanctuary in the Shadows

The closet's full, yet still we shove,
More treasures there than I can love.
A lamp that flickers half the day,
Sits there with a light-hearted sway.

The toilet seat sings out of tune,
While rubber ducks join in a croon.
The kitchen's chaos holds its charm,
As burnt toast serves as a fire alarm.

Old shoes gather dust in pride,
While giggles echo side by side.
In every nook, a memory hangs,
The serpentine of life's weird tangs.

With laughter bursting from each crack,
This quirky place won't turn its back.
It wraps us up with joy untold,
In shadows where our hearts are bold.

Whispering Walls of Belonging

The walls are chattering with glee,
As sticky notes hold secrets free.
The echo of a toddler's cheer,
Turns every frown into a cheer.

Beneath the stairs, a monster dwells,
But all he does is ring our bells.
With tangled cords around my feet,
I trip and laugh—that's quite a feat!

Old photographs make faces wise,
With laughter caught in timeless ties.
A t-shirt worn from days gone by,
Sings loudly, do not say goodbye.

The pillows whisper tales of yore,
And crackling laughter begs for more.
In this abode, pure joy swings wide,
With every mishap as our guide.

Atmosphere of Warmth

In the kitchen, chaos reigns,
Spaghetti's dancing on the panes.
A cat steals fish from off the plate,
While Uncle Joe debates his fate.

Laughter echoes off the walls,
As Auntie trips on endless brawls.
The dog dives in, a furry blur,
And knocks down Grandma's favorite stir.

Mom's chocolate cake, a great divide,
Half for her, and half for pride.
But somehow, it vanishes fast,
With whispers of "You had it last!"

Through laughter, love takes flight,
In every silly, wild delight.
Here, nothing's ever quite the same,
Yet it's all part of this funny game.

Connected Colors

The couch is orange, painted blue,
A tribute to my brother's view.
Socks are lost and couch cushions squished,
In colors that the rainbow wished.

Scattered toys and old board games,
A canvas for our wildest claims.
Each splattered footstep tells a tale,
Of fun-filled days we'll not curtail.

The walls echo with turns of fate,
As one more "oops" we celebrate.
Tangled mess or perfect hue,
It's all a masterpiece, just for you.

With laughter bold and colors bright,
We paint our days from morn till night.
Here's where the chaos finds its beat,
As the bizarre turns bittersweet.

Sanctuary of Dreams

In quiet corners, pillows stack,
A fortress built against the crack.
The whispering winds play peek-a-boo,
As sleepyheads try counting two.

A blanket fort, a grand retreat,
Where dragons fall beneath our feet.
The playing cards become our fate,
While cookies sneak in on a plate.

We spin tall tales of knights and kings,
As laughter flies on paper wings.
Here magic waits behind closed eyes,
In secret spots where chaos lies.

With giggles echoing through the night,
Our dreams unfold in daring flight.
This silly realm, forever gleams,
A sanctuary built of dreams.

Paths That Breathe

Walk through halls of silly sounds,
Where tickle fights and jumpy bounds.
Each creaky step a giggle's spark,
As playful shadows dance till dark.

In every corner lies a quest,
A treasure trove of family jest.
The wardrobe's home to mismatched socks,
And secrets wrapped in silly blocks.

We trace the paths where laughter flows,
With wacky tales the whole world knows.
Through wild ideas and crazy schemes,
We build our bliss in vibrant beams.

These wandering paths, a funny dance,
Where every stumble leads to chance.
Each step together, a joyful breath,
In this adventure, we conquer death.

Bound by the Walls

Four walls surround us tight,
In socks that never match,
We dance like fools in the night,
And hope for no more scratch!

The fridge hums a funny tune,
While leftovers plot a prank,
Spaghetti on a Tuesday noon,
And we must give it thanks!

Chasing dust bunnies with glee,
They hide beneath the chair,
We laugh until we can't see,
But who truly cares where?

The ceiling fan spins with flair,
A whirring joke up high,
Under its watchful stare,
Our laughter fills the sky!

Traveled Paths Inside

Each step echoes through the hall,
As cats plot their next scheme,
In laundry baskets, they sprawl,
Pouncing on the daydream!

The carpets have their stories told,
Of spills and mighty falls,
Mom shakes her head, oh so bold,
As dad claims it's the walls!

Through kitchens we wander with ease,
In search of snacks galore,
Finding crumbs like hidden keys,
Unlocking a tasty score!

In corners, treasures await,
Old toys with nostalgic cheer,
Every inch, we celebrate,
The joys that we hold dear!

Sheltered Journeys

We journey through our living room,
Adventurers on a quest,
With pillows as our safety plume,
And snacks, our trusty vest!

The TV blares our battle cries,
As we dodge the laundry pile,
Magic socks with hidden spies,
Waging war in style!

Grabbing ice cream on the way,
To brave the nightly chill,
With every spoonful we sway,
Fighting sleep, we will.

Finding joy in silly games,
From couch forts to our beds,
In shelter, we spark silly flames,
While laughter fills our heads!

Echoes of Belonging

In every nook, a story hums,
The echoes dance around,
Whiskers twitch as laughter comes,
With antics that astound!

The clocks tick with a quirky beat,
They joke about our time,
As slippers shuffle on our feet,
We search for the next rhyme!

The windows frame our sunlight jokes,
As shadows twist and twirl,
And all our furniture invokes,
A cheer from every swirl!

In the warmth of silly shrieks,
We find our perfect song,
With every chuckle that peaks,
We know where we belong!

Guardian of Dreams

Under the blanket, whispers creep,
Pillows are mountains, laughter leaps.
Monsters retreat, they know their fate,
Snore like a bear, oh it's quite late.

Sock puppets dance on the bedside floor,
Dance like they know there's always more.
A spaghetti dinner, a plate for two,
Just watch out for sauce—it'll stick like glue!

Crayons wielded as swords of might,
A fortress built in the dead of night.
In this land of giggles, we cast a spell,
In our cozy kingdom, all is well.

Dreams are the pillows that float us high,
In this wacky world, we touch the sky.
So pick a star, and give it a wink,
Life's a cartoon, don't you dare blink!

Tranquility Enclosed

In the corner, cats plot and scheme,
Snoozing like kings in a fluffy dream.
Tea's growing cold while we laugh and feast,
A puppy parade, oh what a beast!

Finger paint fights in the living room,
Colors collide, igniting the gloom.
I step on a Lego—oh what a pain!
But giggles erupt like a fizzy rain!

Grandma's recipe smells just divine,
Is it too much salt, or just more wine?
The couch is a ship on a sea of snacks,
Navigate carefully; don't fall through the cracks!

When laughter bubbles like boiling stew,
In our world, a laugh can chase the blue.
So dance in your pajamas, don't think twice,
For tranquility comes with a sprinkle of spice!

Fortress of Affection

Cushions piled high like a fortress grand,
Each soft wall was made by tiny hands.
Sippy cups tip like treasure chests,
Pirates in slippers, we're all guests!

Blankets stretch far, covering the floor,
Underneath, we find adventures galore.
A hidey spot tucked behind the chair,
Where giggles erupt from the challenge to dare.

The cat's an overlord, no need to fight,
She rules with a paw and a sleepy slight.
In our magical lair full of snacks and thrill,
We plot the next scheme without a chill.

The clock ticks softly, time can wait,
With giggles and whispers, we celebrate.
So let the world be wild and aloof,
Here, we're the kings and queens of the roof!

The Spirit of Comfort

When the rain taps soft on the windowpane,
We grab our blanket, invite the brain.
A masterpiece born from crayons and glue,
Who knew that chaos could feel like new?

Chasing the dog, what a sudden twist,
He steals all the socks—did you get the gist?
Under the table, we form a huddle,
In this cozy chaos, we're deeper in muddle.

The spirit of fun fuels the night's delight,
As silly stories take their flight.
Dance like an octopus, wiggle and sway,
In our soft bubble, we'll banish dismay.

So gather round, let the giggling pour,
In this crazy haven, we always want more.
The world outside may be loud and fast,
But in our snug nook, we're free at last!

Spirit of Togetherness

In the kitchen, chaos reigns,
Socks are mixed with flour stains.
Laughter blends with clattering pans,
As we dance in mismatched clans.

Dinner's served, the table's spread,
With more laughter than we've said.
A rolling pin becomes a sword,
In this wildness, joy's restored.

When the cat jumps on the pie,
We all just glance, then start to sigh.
Who told the dog to chase a mouse?
It's never quite a quiet house!

But through the blend of spills and chases,
We find ourselves in all these spaces.
Together we're a jumbled team,
Living life like a wacky dream.

Shades of Comfort

On the couch, we sink so low,
Lost in snacks, the TV's glow.
Remote in hand, the dog demands,
A spot to claim, amidst our plans.

Pajamas rule our lazy days,
In mismatched colors, all the crazes.
Grab some popcorn, who will share?
The couch is claimed, but who would care?

A shelf of books, but no one reads,
We'd rather trade for silly deeds.
Playing games that make us laugh,
Together we're our own comical staff.

Though some may argue, some may tease,
These shades of comfort, always please.
In every giggle, every cheer,
We build our bonds, year after year.

Threads of Resilience

In the morning, cereal spills,
Milk on faces gives us thrills.
Dad's still searching for his shoe,
Mom's already had quite enough, too.

Cushions tossed for pillow fights,
Braces fall in silly plights.
Every spout has a funny tale,
With socks on hands, we'll never fail.

A chore chart full of messy art,
Who did what? It's hard to part.
With markers gone and crayons strayed,
Our home's a mess, but love's displayed.

Through every twist and silly bend,
We find the joy that's hard to mend.
In threads of chaos, we persist,
Embracing laughter, we resist.

Nurtured Spaces

The garden's grown with weeds galore,
A haven full of tales and more.
The neighbors laugh, they shake their heads,
As we plant dreams where doggies tread.

In the attic, treasures lie,
Old toys stacked like they could fly.
Dusty boxes, each holds glee,
Memories wrapped in a riddle spree.

The bathroom's a spa of rubber ducks,
Squeaky sounds burst as joy plucks.
Mommy's hairbrush goes for a ride,
In this circus, we can't hide.

Yet every mess builds up the soul,
In these nurtured spaces, we are whole.
With laughter bright and chaos grand,
We weave a life, hand in hand.

Under the Shelter

In a place where socks go to hide,
And the fridge is our treasure chest,
We dance with the cat on a lopsided ride,
Laugh at the mess, it's all for the best.

The chairs all wobble, the table leans,
Yet we feast on cookies, piles of cheer,
With the dog snoring loud, it's just like dreams,
Every noise is a tune that we hold dear.

Toys scatter like confetti, oh what a sight,
While we giggle and slip on the yogurt spill,
Our living room circus is pure delight,
Who needs a big top, just give us a thrill!

In our little chaos, we find our bliss,
Each corner a story, bizarre and bright,
Join the parade for a silly business,
Under this shelter, all feels just right.

Where Love Grows

In the kitchen, the spatula dances around,
While the blender hums its old favorite tune,
We trade funny faces and make silly sounds,
As the cookies rise like balloons on a June.

Pants on backward, hair in a mess,
We erupt into laughter over a spilled drink,
With a fork as a mic, we sing and we stress,
Knowing this moment is better than you think.

The garden's a jungle, weeds wild and free,
Where we plant our dreams along with the thyme,
We joke about veggies, as silly as can be,
In the midst of the dirt, our joy is in prime.

Love is the glue, it sticks us in place,
With puns and bad jokes, we thrive day to day,
In this space, there's no need for grace,
Just laughter and love, forever at play.

Reflections in the Attic

In the attic, we find treasures so neat,
With dusty old hats and a squeaky chair,
We adorn ourselves like a fancy retreat,
And dance through the cobwebs without a care.

Ghosts of old memories whisper and tease,
While we stumble on boxes of junk from the past,
Each item a riddle, each shadow a breeze,
We laugh at our finds, oh, how they amass!

Under the beams, we plot our next scheme,
To scare all the neighbors with ghastly delight,
Stockpiling phantoms, oh what a dream!
We're the kings of this clutter, ruling the night.

So here's to the attic, our secret domain,
Where giggles and tales intertwine like a vine,
Through laughter and light, we'll never feel pain,
In this quirky kingdom, we flourish just fine.

The Heart's Haven

Amidst the clutter, we forge our retreat,
Where mismatched cushions create our own throne,
We gather our stories, both funny and sweet,
In this cozy embrace, we're never alone.

The dog in the corner snores like a log,
While we argue which movie deserves our night,
With popcorn in hand, we just laugh like a fog,
These moments of joy make everything right.

Through ruffles and giggles, the time flies away,
With socks on the ceiling, we're blessed with the whim,
We live for the hustles, the games that we play,
In our heart's little haven, it's never too dim.

So here's to our haven, our sanctuary bright,
A place filled with warmth, with fun and delight,
Where love and laughter weave through the night,
In our little corner, everything's right.

The Warm Embrace

In a house that's always loud,
Where socks are shoes, and kids are proud.
The dog steals bites from every plate,
And the cat's the king, it's never late.

The fridge is full of mystery,
Leftovers past, an ancient history.
We laugh at meals that got away,
And dance like crazy when kids don't play.

Each room tells tales, some good, some wild,
Of epic fails when we were a child.
With tripping hazards all around,
Laughter erupts, our joyful sound.

From the laughter echoing loud,
To the chaos that makes us proud.
In this messy realm, forever bright,
We find our joy, our pure delight.

Room for Reverie

There's a space where dreams collide,
With pillows soft, it's a wobbly ride.
With teddy bears who rule the night,
And laundry piles that reach new heights.

A hammock swing from wall to wall,
Where gravity seems to take a fall.
We float on air, with giggles so sweet,
In a fortress made of old bedsheets.

Our secret kingdom, so profound,
Where whispering walls share secrets found.
The clock is stuck on playful time,
As we invent our silly rhyme.

In this room of wild delight,
We banish worries, take to flight.
It may not be where quiet reigns,
But oh, the joy that still remains!

The Base of Belonging

In the basement, lids fly high,
Where mops become dragons, oh my!
The treasure hunt for snacks galore,
With tripping stunts on the cold, hard floor.

Hiding spots beneath the stairs,
With notes to friends and silly dares.
The echoing giggles bounce and bloom,
In our fortress, a magical room.

Puzzles scattered and games askew,
Creating worlds for me and you.
Part-time pirates, we search for gold,
With heart and laughter, our tales unfold.

Though darkness lurks and light is thin,
We find the spark that draws us in.
In this haven where we belong,
Laughter is our theme, our song.

Corner of Affection

In the corner where the plants reside,
Sits a chair named 'Where Dreams collide'.
With snacks and drinks piled high in stacks,
And the cat, of course, who never relax.

We share our giggles wrapped in cheer,
As the neighbor's dog barks loud and clear.
With pillow fights that leave a mark,
In our cozy, toasty nook, we embark.

The world outside may seem far away,
But in this corner, we choose to play.
With stories exchanged and dreams that sprout,
We cuddle close, there's never a doubt.

Oh, the warmth of love we gather near,
In laughter, spills, and moments dear.
In this tiny corner, we grow and thrive,
Where echoes of joy keep us alive.

Timeless Ties

In a house where socks go missing,
And the cat thinks it's her throne,
The clutter holds our history,
In laughter, we have grown.

Spilled milk and burnt toast tales,
The spaghetti's gone awry,
Yet every blunder fuels our joy,
As days and nights fly by.

Family photos with funny poses,
Grandpa wearing a hat too tall,
Voices echo in playful banter,
In chaos, we stand tall.

Even the fridge hums our tunes,
With magnets holding our dreams,
In this place of quirky moments,
Life's not always what it seems.

Shelter from the Storm

When rain pours down like laughter,
We cuddle on the couch tight,
Pajamas are our armor,
In this cozy, comedic fight.

The dog steals all the popcorn,
While the kids play hide and seek,
Finding them is quite the challenge,
Their giggles give away their sneak.

Through the thunder and the lightning,
We tell stories with a twist,
Imagination runs wild here,
In a warmth that can't be missed.

So let the tempest rage outside,
Within these walls, joy is born,
As we dance to the storm's rhythm,
In our hearts, no room for scorn.

Shelter of Forgotten Whispers

In corners where dust bunnies gather,
Ghosts of laughter roam free,
Whispers of games long forgotten,
Echo softly through the tea.

Bathtime splash fights, rubber duck wars,
Mom's towel-wrapped as a pirate,
In these tales, we all play parts,
Finding joy in the absurd despite it.

Underneath the creaky staircase,
Secret hideouts have been made,
Hushed conspiracies by the kiddos,
A world in which dreams parade.

Like old dolls with mismatched outfits,
Past adventures still invoke grins,
For in this shelter of nonsense,
The heart's laughter always wins.

The Hearth's Embrace

In the kitchen where smells are magic,
Cookies dance just out of reach,
A sprinkle of flour, a dash of fun,
In this recipe we all teach.

The fireplace flickers with mischief,
S'mores melting in the night,
While tales of yesteryear unravel,
In the warm and flickering light.

The chairs hold stories of visitors,
And board games with rules absurd,
We laugh at our joint blunders,
In this place, we're undeterred.

With every crackle and pop, we gather,
Woven close, our laughter is loud,
For in this embrace, we are family,
A wonderfully silly crowd.

Guardians of the Threshold

With socks on the floor, it's a war zone,

My dog guards his spot like a king on a throne.

The doorbell rings, what an awful sound,

As he barks at the mailman, a foe to be found.

A cat in a box, plotting with glee,

Her secret domain, just her and the spree.

She pounces on shadows, a true ninja bright,

While I trip on the rug, oh, what a delight!

The fridge hums a tune, a melody sweet,

It serenades snacks, quite the tasty feat.

Yet morning's a battle, the coffee's a must,

To face all the chaos, it's brewing with trust.

So here we gather, with laughter and cheer,

In this wild circus, let's spread our good cheer.

For in the madness, love always survives,

With guardians of laughter, our joy surely thrives.

Cradled by Night's Gentle Veil

As the stars check their lists and the moon draws a sigh,

I try to stay up but my eyelids comply.

The couch seems to whisper, "Just have a quick nap,"

While I sink into comfort, oh! What a trap!

A blanket's a fortress, so snug and so warm,

It holds all my dreams safe from any alarm.

The dog curls beside me, a snoring delight,

While visions of snacks dance throughout the night.

With pillows conferring on plans to stay late,

They plot how to keep me from succumbing to fate.

But my bed, it calls softly, with promises sweet,

So I yield to the pull of my mellow retreat.

Each tick of the clock is a giggle, a tease,

While I snuggle up tighter, oh, such cozy ease.

In the hush of the night, goofy dreams come and go,

Cradled in laughter, it's the best kind of show.

The Comfort in Everyday Moments

The kettle whistles a melody bold,
It dances on counters, a sight to behold.
Each cup of warm coffee, a ritual dear,
With cookies for dipping, it's time for cheer.

A mismatched sock, it bears quite the tale,
Of laundry adventures and a lost little trail.
The broom's in the corner, it's taking a rest,
While dust bunnies hop like they're hosting a fest.

Chairs clatter together, a raucous delight,
While family debates whose turn to do right.
And the clock's ticking louder, counting each jest,
Who knew such chaos could feel like a quest?

With laughter as glue, we stick through the fray,
In moments like these, joy will always stay.
So here's to the noise, the quirks and the fun,
In the comfort of chaos, we all are as one.

Echoes of Laughter and Light

In the hallway's embrace, there's a holler and squeal,

As kids plot their mischief with a sneaky appeal.

The cat zooms past, an uninvited guest,

Racing with shadows, she's quite the jest.

The couch is a castle, pillows on guard,

A realm of adventures, it's never too hard.

With blankets as knights, we wage all our wars,

Against tickle attacks and imaginary chores.

Dinner's a circus, a chef's wild display,

As spaghetti's flung high in a noodle ballet.

With sauce on the ceiling, we laugh in delight,

What chaos, what fun—all feels just so right.

In this magical place where we tumble and play,

We find echoes of laughter that brighten the day.

For love's in the chaos, it's always in sight,

With giggles and grins in the soft evening light.

Nestled between Ray and Dusk

A cat sprawls wide on the couch's throne,
Claiming the space as her very own.
While we trip over shoes, scattered around,
She dreams of mice, in her kingdom, unbound.

The fridge hums tales of leftovers past,
While the clock ticks slowly, time stretches vast.
A dance party erupts when the music plays,
Who knew cleaning could have such wild days?

In the kitchen, battles of splatter and sauce,
Each meal a gamble, a game of embossed.
But laughter erupts, and we share our cheers,
Disasters become legends throughout the years.

And as dusk wraps the house in its warm, cozy glow,
We gather to recount the day's utmost show.
In this quirky nest, with its chaos and cheer,
Life feels just right, as the end draws near.

The Quiet Echo of Familiarity

In the laundry room, an odd sock brigade,
Marches to battle, their pairs always frayed.
A toast to the dryer, which eats them with glee,
Leaving us wondering where they could be.

The bathroom mirror reflects silly faces,
As we practice our moves for imaginary races.
Yet every glance carries a giggle or two,
What's a bit of madness when it's me and you?

The squeaky stairs sing songs of surprise,
Each creak a reminder of laughter and sighs.
Every corner holds a secret or tale,
Like that time we tried to bake and set off the hail.

While the coffee pot bubbles, a conspirator's plot,
To wake sleepyheads who've slept way too hot.
In this wacky sanctuary, the fun never fades,
With moments like these, who needs grand parades?

Solace in Closing Doors

Turning the knob, the silence so sweet,
With peace offered up on a fresh, clean sheet.
But soon comes a racket, loud and proud,
As kids rush in, forming a busy crowd.

The dog barks in while we try to recall
What once was a quiet, serene little hall.
Yet every loud entrance and ruckus galore,
We find there's a joy in the uproar we score.

Closing the door? You bet that's a ruse,
As giggles slip in like a sneaky excuse.
Who knew that our space would become so alive,
With each passing moment, the funny vibes thrive?

In this bubbling chaos, we find our sweet grace,
Where comfort lies hidden behind every face.
For all of the mess, and the laughs we adore,
Are treasures we hold, time's closets to explore.

A Tapestry Woven in Love

Threads of the past, in a quilt, we infuse,
Stitched stories of laughter, every shared muse.
We pull crazy pranks, and still laugh 'til we cry,
The tapestry gleams with our moments gone by.

Gather 'round, friends, in this patchwork delight,
Each flap of the fabric recalls our blight.
With stains from the parties and splashes of spritz,
Our colorful chaos is hard to outwit.

And every tale spun holds a giggle or two,
As we duel with the dust bunnies under the shoe.
The kitchen's a frenzy; we dance as we bake,
A recipe's funny, leave it to fate!

As we snuggle up tight in our woven embrace,
The world outside fades; we find our place.
In stitches and laughter, our hearts fill up whole,
This cloth of our life, a mixed bag of soul.

Safe Harbor Thoughts

In a world so wild and wide,
We gather here, no need to hide.
With socks that clash and hair askew,
We laugh at the chaos, just me and you.

A cat on the fridge, what a sight!
While we sip cocoa, feeling just right.
The dishes stack high, a tower of fate,
But we just joke, it can't wait till eight.

An avocado toast, but it's burnt and grey,
You laugh at my cooking, what more can I say?
The takeout menus are a welcome friend,
In this quirky haven, the fun won't end.

So raise a glass to the silly and sweet,
With every mishap, our lives are complete.
In laughter and love, we find our place,
In this crazy ship, we embrace the space.

Tapestry of Togetherness

Stitches of laughter weave through the halls,
Where jokes echo loudly, and friendship calls.
The dog steals the pizza straight off the plate,
While we scramble around, it's never too late.

From board games of war to snacks on the floor,
We gossip and giggle, always wanting more.
Your dance moves are awful, yet full of delight,
As we twirl under lights, feeling so bright.

The laundry's a mountain, oh my, what a sight!
But we choose to ignore it, it'll be fine tonight.
With ice cream in hand and pajamas askew,
We snicker and snack until dreams ensue.

In this patchwork of joy, we create every day,
With a wink and a grin, come what may.
Together we bond, with chaos in view,
This tapestry of love, forever renew.

The Cornerstone of Us

Our fortress is built on leftovers and cheer,
With a six-pack of laughter that stands ever near.
The coffee pot brews, oops! It spilled on the floor,
But wait, there's more! I can't take it no more!

The slippers are mismatched; what a sight to behold,
As I trip over blankets, your stories unfold.
In the chaos, we find little nuggets of gold,
In mishaps we cherish, a tale to be told.

When the neighbors all stare as we dance in the rain,
We twirl and we spin, forgetting the pain.
We're silly and goofy, and that's just our way,
In this cornerstone crazy, forever we'll stay.

So here's to the laughter, the quirks that endear,
In this sweet little chaos, we know we're sincere.
With every mad moment, through life's little fuss,
We carve out our path, the true cornerstone of us.

Whispers of the Past

Echoes of giggles float through the air,
As we reminisce, lost in laughter's flare.
The photos, they shout with a story or two,
Of antics we pulled that still crack up the crew.

The time you thought broccoli was a tree,
You danced around shouting, 'Look at me!'
We baked a cake that flopped like a lead,
Yet the memories we made are never misread.

With socks on our hands, we put on a show,
Each moment, a treasure, in sunshine's glow.
For every bold blunder, and each silly fight,
The whispers of past always bring pure delight.

So let's raise our glasses, to the years we've amassed,
To syrupy mornings and lessons unsurpassed.
In this lively abode, where the heart found its cast,
We laugh and we love, embracing the past.

Refuge of Familiarity

In socks that match, yet clash in hue,
We dance around, with dinner due.
The cat's the boss; we obey his rule,
While trying to find the lost TV remote.

Spilled some juice on the living room rug,
The dog just snores and gives a shrug.
Mom laughs hard; Dad can't keep straight,
As we untangle our dinner plate fate.

A comedy show at the dining table,
Where every mishap is a fable.
We toast with milk in plastic cups,
To living the dream, with all our goof-ups.

When the doorbell rings, it's Auntie Sue,
With cookies that look too good to chew.
We feast on laughs, and stories abound,
In this familiar refuge, where joy is found.

The Shelter of Memories

Grandpa's stories, like wildflower seeds,
Sprout laughter and joy in hilarious deeds.
The dog's old bed becomes a trampoline,
While mice play tag where dust bunnies preen.

Mom's cooking experiments, a daring game,
Whose smoke alarms are never quite the same.
In the chaos, we share silly, sweet,
As dad wears aprons—an odd fashion feat.

Chasing shadows with silly dance moves,
Our living room turns to light-hearted grooves.
In corners, the echoes of laughter remain,
Every crack and creak, a familiar refrain.

As we gather 'round, tales spinning fast,
The best times are those that proudly last.
Wrapped in ridiculous warmth, we find,
This shelter of memories, forever entwined.

Embracing the Hearth

On winter nights, the fire pops loud,
We roast marshmallows, feeling quite proud.
The cat rolls by, snagged on a sock,
While siblings giggle, it's quite the shock!

Baked goods cooling by the window sill,
My brother sneaks one, much against my will.
We argue and giggle, a funny old show,
As icing drips from the last brownie dough.

With piles of blankets built to the sky,
We plot secret missions, oh me, oh my!
The hearth our stage for imagination's cheer,
Where the wildest of dreams seem so near.

Embracing the laughter as the sun goes down,
Our little paradise, our cozy town.
In the glow of the fire, we delightfully play,
Creating memories that won't fade away.

Nestled in Warmth

Cousins collide on the couch like a wave,
In a pile of laughter, who will be brave?
The cookies, they vanish, as if by a spell,
With crumbs and giggles, we know it too well.

A race for the bathroom during game night,
Who can hold it? What a silly sight!
We mock and we laugh, it's a grand ol' time,
In these absurd moments, the joy's at its prime.

The TV's on, but who's really watching?
We're sharing our secrets and laughing non-stop.
With cushions as shields, we engage in our fight,
To see who can meme the best in that light.

Nestled in warmth, with hearts all aglow,
These funny little tales, in memories flow.
In our quirky bubble, we twist and twirl,
Creating a haven, our merry world.

The Inheritance of Love

In the attic, I found Uncle Bob's hat,
Dusty and old, I wonder what's that?
A hidden treasure, or just a silly joke?
With feathers and sequins, oh what a bloke!

The couch in the corner? It squeaks with delight,
It's seen more rom-coms than Netflix at night.
I swear it sighs when I settle down,
Mocking my choices, the fabric, the brown!

Picture frames filled with faces we know,
Who are these strangers? I really don't know.
They smile and they wave from the dust-covered glass,
As if they're waiting for me to pass!

The fridge has opinions on what I should eat,
With magnets so bright, it's more than a treat.
"Leftover pizza? Not today," it seems to say,
"Why not some healthy kale—make it snappy, okay?"

Nest of Serenity

In the corner, there's a chair that creaks,
Where thoughts and snores mingle for weeks.
Add the cat with her regal pose,
Claiming it all, dozing with her nose.

The kitchen's always bustling with sounds,
Pots and pans clash in jolly rounds.
Spaghetti dances off the stove in glee,
While the blender wants to steal the show, you see!

Laundry piles high, like a mountain of fluff,
Colors entwined, and it's getting quite tough.
"Where's that sock?" I frequently shout,
Guess it's off on adventures, no doubt!

We're all a bit quirky, that much is clear,
Celebrating chaos with loads of cheer.
Inside this nest of oddity and mirth,
We find our joy, our laughter, our worth.

Heartstrings in the Framework

In the hallway, pictures hang out of line,
Creating an art piece that's simply divine.
Each family snapshot, a goofy display,
With Uncle Joe's mustache making fun of the day.

The creaky stairs lead to stories untold,
With each step I take, new tales unfold.
Ghosts of the past give a chuckle or two,
Whispering secrets that only we knew.

The ceiling fan spins like it's flown off the track,
Chasing its dreams while I'm chasing a snack.
It wobbles and shakes till it finally stops,
But it's my constant companion, it never drops!

Heartstrings twinkle in every creak and sigh,
They laugh and they play as the years drift by.
In every corner, adventure's afoot,
As we dance over socks and the odd little boot.

Reflections of Us

The bathroom mirror reflects my wild hair,
With toothpaste splatters that show I don't care.
Each morning a circus, a riotous game,
Caught in a shampoo bottle's fame!

In the spare room, a collection of hats,
Each one a story, like cats without mats.
Feathers and fedoras, too silly to wear,
Yet they bring sunshine to this old, blank square.

In the garden, gnomes have a party at night,
Dancing with daisies in colorful flight.
They celebrate birthdays we never hold dear,
While squirrels throw confetti—what a raucous cheer!

Reflections so silly, they sum up our days,
Through laughter and joy in the strangest of ways.
Here's to the memories, both big and small,
In this glorious chaos, we truly stand tall!

Silent Sanctuary

In the corner sits a cat,
Who claims the chair like that.
When I bring a cup of tea,
She gives me a look, how dare she?

Dust bunnies run in their dance,
While I trip and take a chance.
The fridge hums a silly tune,
While leftovers plan their coup.

Each corner holds a secret snack,
A chocolate bar I can't bring back.
Under cushions, crumbs abound,
It's a feast that's never found.

A quiet space with echoes loud,
Where my thoughts wear a silly shroud.
With every creak the floorboard gives,
I laugh at how every silence lives.

Hearthstone Whispers

Wooden floors squeak with delight,
As my socks engage in a fight.
The couch is a fortress of fluff,
Where even the strongest can't be tough.

A blanket fort rises, a grand display,
With pillows stacked like a buffet.
The aroma of burnt popcorn wafts,
As I watch my plans take odd drafts.

Dancing shadows in the evening glow,
Pretend they're friends in a lively show.
The thermostat fights a stubborn chill,
As I nibble on snacks against my will.

Jokes fly like paper planes around,
In this silly, cozy battleground.
Every corner has laughter's echo,
Amongst the dust, a great good show.

The Comfort of Shadows

The light flickers like a candle's song,
As the toaster croaks, it won't be long.
Mismatched socks crawl up the stairs,
Awaiting the saga that no one cares.

Chairs are jigsaw puzzles of fate,
Finding legroom I contemplate.
The TV yells with a wild cheer,
While I just nod and pretend to hear.

Naps on the couch form a cozy art,
Where time slows down, and naps restart.
Blankets layer like fluffy hills,
Embracing my dreams and eccentric thrills.

Each sigh of the floor brings a laugh,
As I measure the snacks in a gaffe.
In shadows, the weirdness has an appeal,
Turning mundanity into a surreal deal.

Embrace of Four Walls

Four walls cradle my daily show,
Where socks disappear in a rogue flow.
The fridge holds secrets, oh what a stash,
While my dreams often turn into a crash.

The bathroom plays host to grand plans,
For the epic struggles with rubber bands.
Toothpaste battles for rightful acclaim,
In this arena of a brush's fame.

Curtains flutter like gossiping friends,
Sharing secrets till the daylight ends.
Books stack high like a tower bold,
Each page a story worth more than gold.

With laughter echoing, we find our place,
In this goofy, warm, and familiar space.
Where silliness thrives beneath the light,
And every day feels hilariously right.

Timeless Stories Told in Silence

In the attic, dust bunnies roam,
Laughing at the stories alone.
A chair that creaks with every thought,
Whispers of battles, time forgot.

Books stacked high, like towers fall,
Each page a tale that starts to call.
The cat's on guard, with a watchful stare,
She's convinced every ghost is out there.

Old clocks tick as if they know,
Of secrets that the shadows show.
A sock that vanished, a shoe with holes,
Unraveling history – oh, how it rolls!

In the corners where echoes hide,
Laughter jumps, refuses to bide.
Each crevice, a memory, a raucous cheer,
Timeless stories that we hold dear.

In the Company of Old Photographs

Snapshots pinned on the wall,
Smiling faces, having a ball.
Uncle Joe with his crazy hat,
Dancing with auntie, oh look at that!

Mom's hairstyle defies all fate,
What was cool then? A mystery, mate!
The dog in shades, striking a pose,
Funny how time's humor just grows.

Each flash tells a tale from the past,
With questionable fashion that didn't last.
Cousins who found mud on their shoes,
Laughing so hard, we'd never lose.

In sepia tones, the moments flare,
Echoing laughter fills the air.
Every picture's a giggle, a tease,
Forever taken, if you please!

Refuge in the Calm of Twilight

As daylight fades, the shadows play,
The couch turns into a sacred bay.
With popcorn piled as tall as dreams,
We settle in, ready for midnight schemes.

The TV flickers with ghosts from the past,
Old reruns where time moves fast.
With a blanket fortress, we laugh and sigh,
Under the safety of the evening sky.

The lamp invites, with a warm, soft glow,
Spilling secrets that only we know.
Even the clock ticks in a jesting tune,
Tick-tock and giggles, we float like a balloon.

In the twilight calm, worries take flight,
Wrapped in a glow that feels just right.
With chuckles and whispers, we claim the night,
In our cozy nook, every wrong feels right.

The Spaces That Hold Us Tight

Corners that cradle our silly dreams,
Where laughter bubbles and sunlight beams.
The kitchen hums with flavors new,
A dance of spices and a joke or two.

Hallways echo with playful shouts,
As little feet race and bounce about.
Each room a treasure, with memories sown,
A tapestry woven, a life that's grown.

The swing on the porch sways with glee,
As stories unfold under the old oak tree.
A croaked frog joins in the fun,
It's a duet of mischief, never done.

The spaces around us know our tales,
From whispered secrets to lighthearted fails.
With every heartbeat, they weave us close,
In these silly bounds, we love the most.

Roost of Togetherness

In the nest of laughter, we poke and tease,
Shoes piled high, like messy trees.
Dinner's a battle, who'll win the prize?
Last night's leftovers bring comic surprise.

Cats chase shadows, dogs steal the chair,
Socks in the fridge? We're quite the pair!
Tickle fights echo, giggles galore,
Under this roof, there's never a bore.

Silly debates on who lost the game,
Pasta or pizza? We're all the same.
With each little quirk, our hearts intertwine,
Together we frolic, our spirits align.

The wildest of tales are never too far,
Trust in the chaos, it's who we are.
In our cozy quarters, laughter ignites,
Every day's antics feel oh-so-right.

Safe Nook Dreams

Nestled in cushions, we drift and sway,
Chasing wild dreams till the end of the day.
Blankets become forts, a secret domain,
Imagination runs wild like a runaway train.

Pizza in pajamas, we munch and play,
Lost in a giggle, we just can't stay gray.
Silly sock puppets put on a show,
'Tis a grand performance on the floor below.

A cat in a crown, a dog in a tie,
Rules of the universe? We let them fly.
Pillow fights scatter our giggling crew,
As love fills the air, dreams come true.

In our nook of joy, the whimsical reigns,
Joining our quirks, it's what entertains.
So here's to the antics, the cozy esteem,
In this safe haven, we live our dream.

Cherished Corners

In the corners where clutter takes its place,
We find our treasures, our goofy space.
Cereal for dinner, and who needs cutlery?
Messy adventures are part of our history.

Bouncing on couches, we laugh and collide,
Laughter erupts like popcorn, a tide.
Squeaky chairs join in on our fun,
Each moment rambunctious, never just one.

Oh, the socks that go missing, what a delight,
Hiding under cushions, out of our sight.
Sticky fingers on walls, we'll claim,
Every little blunder feels part of the game.

We dance without music, with moves oh-so-rad,
Inventing new steps, some silly, some bad.
In these cherished spots, all craziness flows,
Together forever, as laughter grows.

Secrets in the Eaves

Whispers of giggles float under the beams,
Sharing our secrets, plotting our schemes.
What's that noise? Oh, mom's on a call,
Shhh... we're ninjas, we can't let her fall.

In the attic, a treasure of dust bunnies lay,
Each little creature has something to say.
With shadows that dance, our imaginations steer,
We're the kings and queens, no room for fear.

When dinner's a drama, and chaos ensues,
Spaghetti fights follow, and laughter ensues.
Trips to the fridge feel like quests of great fame,
In the land of our kingdom, we live up our name.

As twilight descends, we gather and beam,
In the eaves where the sunlight does gleam.
With our hearts full of joy, we seal our decree,
The secrets we share bind us like a tree.

www.ingramcontent.com/pod-product-compliance
Lightning Source LLC
Chambersburg PA
CBHW060110230426
43661CB00003B/147